362.3
AND

3,157
$6.95

P9-APZ-213

	DATE DUE		

AUTHOR: ANDERS, REBECCA
TITLE: A LOOK AT MENTAL
RETARDATION

A look at
MENTAL RETARDATION

Lerner Awareness Series

A look at
MENTAL RETARDATION

photographs by **Maria S. Forrai**

text by **Rebecca Anders**

foreword by Muriel Humphrey

Lerner Publications Company, Minneapolis

The publisher wishes to thank the Children's Health Center, the Minneapolis Public School System, the Pilot City Regional Center, and the Roseville Public School System for their cooperation in the preparation of this book.

The camera used was a single-lens reflex Bronica, 2¼" x 2¼" negatives. The text is set in 18 point Baskerville, and the book paper is 80# Black-and-White Gloss Enamel.

LIBRARY OF CONGRESS CATALOGING IN PUBLICATION DATA

Forrai, Maria S.
  A look at mental retardation.

  (Lerner Awareness Series)
  SUMMARY: Text and photographs describe problems faced by people who are mentally handicapped.

  1. Mentally handicapped—Pictorial works—Juvenile literature. [1. Mentally handicapped] I. Anders, Rebecca. II. Title. III. Title: Mental retardation.

HV3004.F76 1976   362.3   75-38466
ISBN 0-8225-1303-X

Manufactured in the United States of America

International Standard Book Number: 0-8225-1303-X
Library of Congress Catalog Card Number: 75-38466

4 5 6 7 8 9 10 90 89 88 87 86 85 84 83 82 81

Muriel Humphrey talks about Mental Retardation...

Let us get the message out and clear—most of our mentally retarded citizens can learn and attend school. They can work. They can reside in the community. They can live a so-called normal lifespan. Very simply, they are people with needs like our own.

There is no more important place to begin in changing public misconception about the retarded than in our schools, where those with this handicap must have the chance to participate, to have their talents acknowledged, and to be accepted by other children and adults.

Therefore, I am pleased to commend this book to teachers and students with the hope that by carrying its message to others we can help assure a new day in public attitude and receptiveness toward all who suffer from the affliction of mental retardation.

Muriel Humphrey

Mrs. Hubert H. Humphrey

Intelligence, or the ability to learn, is very important in our society. Most of us want to do the best we can with the talents that we have been given.

Some people are unusually intelligent—they are often described as gifted. These people are able to write music, design skyscrapers, or program computers.

But a few people have trouble learning even the simplest tasks. They may not be able to tie their shoelaces or to count.

When people have trouble learning what most children can learn, they may not have normal intelligence. People with subnormal intelligence are called *mentally retarded.*

Mental retardation has many causes. Mothers who have serious accidents or illnesses during their pregnancies can give birth to mentally retarded children.

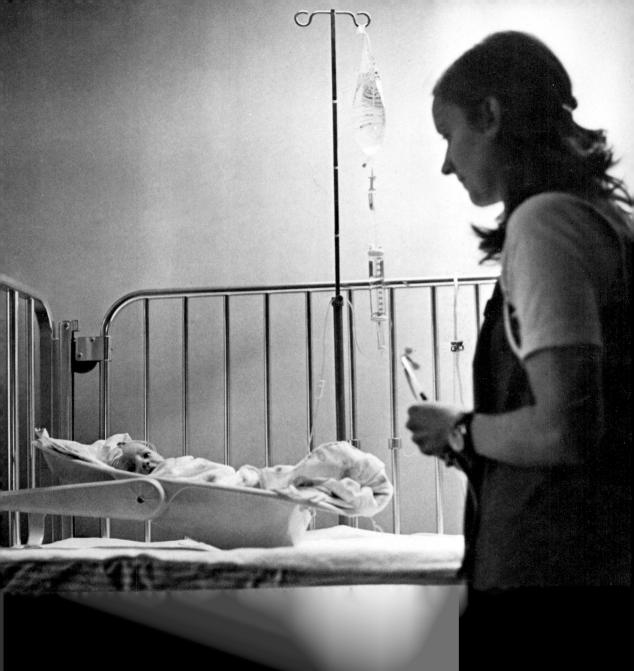

And sometimes babies suffer brain damage during birth. A serious illness or a lack of good food can also injure the brain of a growing child.

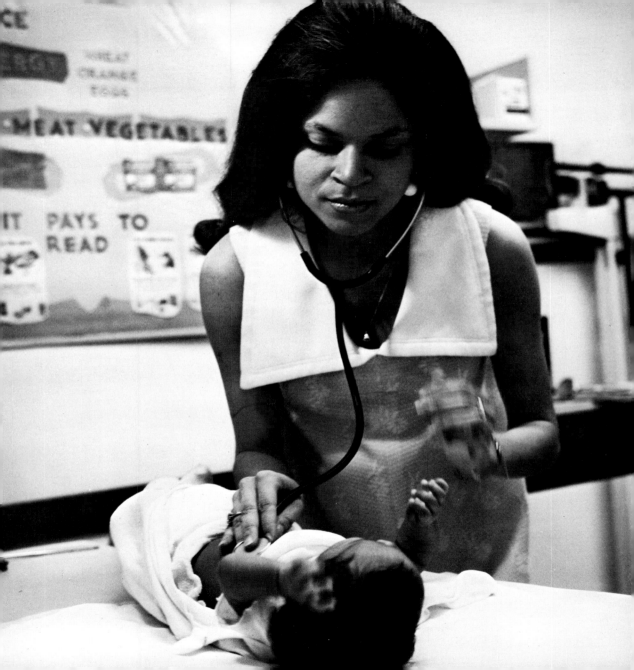

Another kind of retardation may occur in children who receive little attention or care. When there are very few chances to learn, a child's mental growth may be limited.

Intelligence tests can be used to discover whether a child is mentally retarded.

Many doctors and teachers have a special interest in mentally retarded people. They can help each one to learn and grow.

Almost all retarded people are able to learn, though they learn more slowly than most people.

Many mentally retarded people are able to learn trades and earn their own livings. Some can even be taught to read and write.

Even when mentally retarded people are doing well in school or at work, they know that they are somehow different. Like everyone else, they need to be liked and accepted.

When surrounded by people who care about them, the mentally retarded can lead happy, useful lives.

If there are mentally retarded students in your school, you can do much to help them. With friendship and encouragement, your mentally retarded classmates will find it easier to learn.

Perhaps you can even help your retarded friends to discover the special skills and talents that they, too, have to offer.

About the Artist

Maria S. Forrai makes her living by taking photographs. "Photography is a family tradition with me," she explains. "In Hungary, where I was born, my mother became a very good portrait photographer. And here in the United States, my husband and I are establishing ourselves as architectural photographers. Designers and builders hire us to take dramatic pictures of their schools, shopping centers, and office buildings." In addition to the work she does with her husband, Maria likes to photograph people. "I try to show the reality of people's lives in my photographs," says Maria. "I want to capture what they are thinking and feeling."

Many of Maria's photographs have won prizes. They have been on display in Leipzig, Germany, as well as in Budapest, Hungary. More recently, her work has been shown at the University of Illinois and at the University of Minnesota. Maria lives with her husband and two children in St. Paul, Minnesota.